Beyond the Bones

Neil Carpathios

FUTURECYCLE PRESS

Mineral Bluff, Georgia

Published by FutureCycle Press
Mineral Bluff, Georgia, USA

ISBN 978-1-938853-25-8

for Alexandra and Jonathan
for my mother

Contents

I

II

III

I

Workers for the Lord

Cocked for sudden release,
the spirit into the body
is fed, is implanted,
is rigged. The workers
factor in desire,
loneliness, longing; the need
for symmetry, for beauty,
for meaning. They bury deep
the as-yet undiscovered lesson
that we must lose to have.
They sketch the intricate street map
of the heart, purposely draw it
with dead ends, blurred lines,
no key. They insert,
at the center, a tiny complete
self that exists only in theory.
They cover it with layers of false selves,
with bones, organs, muscle, blood.
Sometimes, at the end of a shift,
tired and ready to quit,
just before the skin
they add too much of one thing,
not enough of another.
They go home to celestial husbands, wives,
complain about their day
on the line. They drink and sit staring
out at the moon, something even they love,
feeling guilty having to booby-trap
each package: With sickness, death,
the submission to time. With how the body thinks,
and the soul can be touched,
confusing us. With how roses by the wall
of battered bricks have something to say,

but not for human ears. With how we can get close
to naming a thing, but not close enough,
as when wind shakes rainwater from leaves
making a sound like hands clapping,
but not exactly.

April Fools

The vandals stole the street signs,
even the names from our mail boxes,
so for one April Wednesday in the twenty-first century

we didn't live anywhere and for those driving through
our humble little neighborhood
we didn't really exist.

I stood on my front porch watching the mail truck
circling the block like an Alzheimer's patient
trying to remember or a lost dog hoping to

pick up a scent. We became interchangeable
like pieces on a checkerboard:
I got Feldman's *Playboy* magazine,

he got my rejected poems. It was as if God
wanted to see just how attached we were
to who we thought we were, as if He

was conducting a little experiment,
looking down watching the confusion
from His fluffy recliner as He munched

bowl after bowl of popcorn. Or maybe
He got tired of all our bickering,
lies, especially the killing, and wanted

us to realize how much the same we are
when we peel off name tags and how
in love with name tags we've become.

Everyone came out of their houses,
stood in their yards, shaking
their heads, squinting and walking

around, exploring for some evidence,
staring at the bricks, the driveways,
the trees and each other as if we had

just hatched from an egg
and by instinct started over
from scratch, taking in the world

piece by piece, like baby chicks,
like infants crawling, like cavemen
and women learning a new language.

The Body of Christ

In Sunday School the teacher said communion
is the body of Christ so when I put the cube
of bread inside my mouth and swallowed,
his arms and legs, his heart, his private
parts unfolded, blossomed in my belly like
sea monkeys dropped in water coming alive.
I remember the taste of blood,
an eyelash caught between my teeth,
his flowering flesh expanding
till it reached the boundary of
my skin. It shaped itself, a replica
of me. I could feel the crunching moan
of organs, bones, and meat, the fury of
some holy thing I was told to love
crushing me from inside.

The Egg

Impatient for it to hatch,
every morning I'd rush
to where it lay on grass
by the mailbox,
nudge it with a stick
to wake the baby I pictured
curled up sleeping,

but it never moved.

Once I heard a tick
inside the shell
I pictured was the chick
flicking on a lamp
to read his little instruction book
on how to be what he'd be: a bird.

Chapter One: *Catching Worms*
Chapter Two: *How to Build a Nest*
Chapter Three: *How to Recognize Windows and Not Smash Glass*

And so on.

My sister scolded leave it,
but I got tired and on the fourth day took
a rock and mashed it into yellow goo,
then poked through embryonic slime
and bits of broken shell
determined to find the book

every living thing must read.

Cruelty

We shot a squirrel with a slingshot,
which fell out of the tree,
picked the stunned thing up
and stuck him half-alive
in the freezer then later
watched him thaw, stumbling
drunk. We stuffed firecrackers
in a frog's mouth,
watched it explode into pieces.
With a magnifying glass
we scorched ants on the drive,
watched them sizzle and pop.
We found a wounded sparrow
in a field, tied a string around
its neck, watched it try to fly
as if on a leash. We super-
glued a mouse to a kite
and watched it terrified
dip and soar.
      I wonder if
my friends, wherever they are,
sometimes remember
how we laughed,
called ourselves
mad scientists, Nazis,
how each night our assignment
was to come up with
new experiments.
      When we die will all the dead
creatures we tortured ask why?
Will they ask what we learned,
in a darkness that one day
will swallow us?

Will we answer,
as when our parents
caught us, sheepishly grin,
stare down at our feet
and say nothing?
          We left behind the furry
skittering, the tiny
toothed and clawed
and did what boys do:
We grew into men
and moved on to bigger things.

Hide and Seek

When all our secret places were used,
we found a new way to fool each other:
we grew adult bodies
to hide inside.

        The child
has been hidden so long,
he's desperate to be found.

       If you sit in silence
for long periods
you can feel him
with hands and feet
against your inner walls,
kicking, punching, scratching.

      Maybe someday he'll push
the pieces of you apart
and emerge—

     and there among bits
of your broken body
you'll stare at each other,
embrace, talk about old times,
begin gluing you back together.

Dear Future

How are you?
Are you remembering today?
Me, sitting here in my body picturing
what you look like as you look
over your shoulder back at me?

I could just sit here and wait till I become you,
which is what I'm doing,
although usually I distract myself
by keeping busy.

It is good of you to wait for me
like a big brother purposely walking slowly
so I might catch up with short legs.

I should admit, I've been in love with you
from the beginning. Sometimes I dream
that you primp in a mirror, place pillows
just so, rearrange furniture, as anxiously in love
as I seem to be.

Then I wake up. You're the fake rabbit
and I'm the greyhound racing round and round
the track.

I'm not complaining. I know I'll never have you,
even though we belong to each other,
soul mates.

Anyway,
just thought I'd say hello.

(You're reading this before I'm even finished.
You really do care).

Being Human

What I like best about being a person
is being alone aware of my aloneness
        and that other people are somewhere else.

        Then, each thought I have is an object
across the room I can measure my distance
away from.

Like saying something and watching the words
fly from my mouth and flutter away.
    I can't bring them back.
They love their freedom and find some hidden nest
inside a person's ear or in a crevice in a rock
    or deep inside a cloud.

You understand; you notice space.

You think: I am *here,* my words are *there.*
You look at words in your head, start to measure:
    The only difference between *here* and *there* is a *t,*

    and a prayer. Admit: You often pray

to be somewhere you're not. Somewhere with someone
you're not with. Or somewhere alone aware of your aloneness.

The Obvious Never Tips His Hat

Did I fall through a trapdoor in the sky?

Or is that the residue of too many cartoons?

Either way, here I am.

Are my bones tinker-toys someone assembled?

      (There you go, my guardian angel gripes.)

My heart is a yoyo someone plays with inside my chest.
My tongue is a red carpet I roll out for my lover.

Sometimes my shadow wears riot gear.
Sometimes my shadow hides from me for days.

Each night I hang my face on a hook by my bed,
search for my original face,
      the face I had before my parents were born.

Some nights I find it;
by morning I vomit me
      like a bulimic mosquito.

Nothing starts over and nothing stops ending.

Which brings me back to the sky and the trapdoor—

      (my guardian angel rolls his eyes)

    and those stars I know are wondering how long they have left
on their astral death row.

Autopsy

Perhaps I was too young
to see it,
but they let me.
On the seventh floor
of the hospital
in the lab
where I worked one summer.
She was blond and beautiful,
stretched out naked,
the fortune cookie
of her body waiting
to be cracked open.
I remembered Biology
dissecting frogs,
there was no buried treasure,
but this was a person.

The doctors played with organs,
bones, blood,
but I looked down
into her, saw footprints
which led so far and deep
until they reached the edge
of a beach
under orange sky
where they disappeared
as if she went into
an ocean.

The doctors determined the cause
of death was pneumonia,
which they explained was like
drowning. I knew she went
for a swim forever.

I still wonder what her fortune was,
what secret message each of us carries
slipped into us
before we're slipped into our mothers.

Was she impatient,
deciding to see for herself,
even searching the bottom
of her ocean, and did she ever find it?

Factoid #1: The Hummingbird is the Only Bird that Can Fly Backwards

If he were a man—say, me—
would this power translate to pressing a rewind button
under my shirt?

The rain pours up, the sun rises at night,
flower petals curl and close swallowed by the stem
and the stem shrinks into seed.

The TV says a man jumped off the Empire State Building.
I press my button and, voila, the man's eyeballs fly
back into his reassembled skull,

his blood flows back into his body on cement,
his teeth like tiny white moths float back to their nest
in his mouth, and his arms and legs reassemble

as he rises to the ledge then moves back through
whatever pain brought him to this spot.
I watch his wife come back, unpack the suitcase,

unwrite the Dear John letter—*I realize now
I never really loved you* sucked back into the pen.
I move him back to the day he and his wife first

made love, their faces twisting, every muscle tense
at the moment of release, *Oh god Oh god* like birds
pulled back into their mouths. I go further still

to their first kiss, to the moment they first glimpse
each other in a room. I watch his bald spot darken,
his pot belly flatten. I watch him turn into the boy

with the black eye and crooked ball cap, the toddler
gumming a slice of bread. Then slime-covered,
he slides back into his mother's womb,

her legs close up, her belly rises again. I look hard
at his squinched-up face and see he is eager
and hungry—like any thing about to be born—

for the life that is his, however short or long,
his tiny head thumping the wet inner walls,
his pearl-sized fingers searching for a switch.

The Narcissist Trapped in Third Person

He dreams of an operation that will free the buried I.

Searched and searched but found no surgeons who knew a procedure.

Tried to operate on himself but it hurt too much.

Is tired of looking in the mirror and seeing someone else.

Shrinks were the worst, trying to get him to accept his condition.

He has tried to peel off his face which he swears is a silly mask.

He falls in love, jealous of the man the woman says she misses,
which is him, which is not him, so he always breaks it off.

He believes his life is some god's dirty trick.

He dreams in first person but always wakes back in third.

He writes poems about himself, like this one, wanting pity
before he dies and flies out of his body.

Instead of Writing a Poem about Writing a Poem, I Step Outside and Smell the Air

Rain-choked worms like severed veins
twist on the sidewalk.
I picture their tiny rooms
underground flooded, their miniature
stoves, books, pots and pans
bobbing up and down,
their furniture like rafts floating.
I wonder when the rain stops
if they find their way back
to assess damages.
Do they weep at the loss?
Do they scavenge to find their sopping
items? Do they build a new home,
starting over from scratch?
Do they talk about the tragedy,
have film footage and interviews
like hurricane victims on TV?
Do they blame it on some god
who maybe was bored and ornery,
who needed a little excitement?
I watch them carefully to see if they wiggle
frantically to find their washed-out husbands,
wives, sons and daughters. As a boy
I'd run outside, scoop them up,
house them in a jar. I'd give them
plenty of dirt and grass to keep them safe
until I took them fishing where I'd pierce them
in the head or heart with a barbed hook and see them
bleed and ooze and writhe. Then I let them slowly die
underwater, pray some even bigger creature
would finish them off. I sniff and smell

their nakedness. Smell concrete, damp soil,
drops exploding all around me. I go back inside
and start to scribble words, label things,
wonder if my ears could hear
would their screams be translatable.

Factoid #2: Men Are Six Times More Likely to Be Struck by Lightning than Women

Is it because men are, generally, taller?
Or do we have more fillings,
mouths full of metal?
Or are we just more reckless and stupid?

It rains, a rumbling
in the clouds
as I sit on my stoop pondering—

and, yes,
my neighbor Bob, to my left,
still pushes his mower,
ignoring the first flashes
like veins in God's forehead,

and my other neighbor, Jim,
starts out for a jog,
iPod ear-pods piping, I imagine,
ACDC into his head.

Does God like to punish us
for thinking we run the show
while our women scrub the floor,
stir the stew,
fret over hip size
and ignore our chest-thumping machismo?

Each time another bolt french-fries a golfer
on some hill,
I imagine God drawing a line
on a chalkboard,
keeping score,

thinking to Himself,
nice shot.

The sky darkens.
More kabooms and flashes.

I get up and go inside
to find my lover
whom I will hold
in my mortal arms.

Pressing Buttons

I turn the channel as they start
to talk about the abducted little girl.
How she was playing right outside
her house and disappeared and now
they think they've found her body
in a field. I'd rather watch the stupid
sitcom where the family dog talks
and outsmarts the humans. I'd rather
watch the game show where contestants
try to guess the price of furniture.
I'd rather watch reruns of *Gomer Pyle,*
listening to his backwoods hick drawl.
I'd rather watch the weather guy
waving his arms and talking excitedly
about six inches of snow
as if it is some tragedy about to occur.

Any Given Sunday

In the street the neighbor kid
holds a cap pistol
to his head,

the old man next door
who lost his wife
counts on his fingers.
        Maybe counting days or hours
   or kisses.

       The retarded girl jumps
from her swing to go whisper
something to her pet brick.
        She caresses it like a human cheek.

In a hammock between two trees
a dog snores and dreams
       the power of a misplaced decimal.

A father in a garage clanks tools—
       let's unzip him:

suitcases full of diamonds,
naked women on pedestals.

       All the trees bend lower
to eavesdrop on the conversations
of ants.

       The old man holds his face in his hands.

       The kid with the pistol pulls the trigger.

Hunger

I sleep and my heart stays awake:
it looks out through the bars of my ribs,
through meat, bones, skin,
with x-ray eyes.
It is looking for something to feed it,
even now, despite a whole day's gorging
on my beautiful children, the woman breathing
rhythmically at my side, memories and the aftershock
of memories, clouds, trees, birds.

Sometimes I wake in the middle of the night
and catch it in the act. It says it's sorry,
but I know the heart is a liar and will wait
for as long as it takes for me to drift off again.

II

We Feed Him

The violent extraction of love from the body
is what God's workers are instructed

to carry out. They line up and empty the love
from great buckets into a vat where God hoards

the purest feeling to fill his goblet to drink.
The workers are expert, scanning Earth

from cloud perches, spotting just when
to swoop down invisibly.

They watch men and women who think
they have locked the love deep

inside chambers of their hearts.
They wait for the second when mortals,

like children who collect stones or shells,
take out their treasures to finger, marvel over,

inspect. Then it is easy, a matter of timing.
But sometimes for stubborn ones the workers

need corkscrews and pliers. Which is messy.
We paint them with wings and haloes,

these thieves. But their hands are blood-stained.
Sometimes we can feel their hands.

Work

When you've been alone too long,
the empty mailbox means more to you
than it should. You hover by windows
every day looking out at the little red

flag, waiting and waiting.
You look at the trees like so many
raised hands in a classroom,
nature's way of saying *Here I am,*

knowing they're really just trees
feeling no need to fight for your
attention. You look forward to
junk emails whose invitations

signal someone is thinking
of you, offering to cleanse your colon
or enhance your libido or tell you
the secrets of becoming a millionaire.

You listen to floors creaking,
imagine bones of the house
hidden behind plaster, like you,
developing arthritis. You study

furniture the way you would
sleeping animals, wonder if
when you're around they play
dead and when you leave the room

they wink at each other and breathe.
Even the fly that got in you welcome
and watch—as he backs up, charges
over and over, ticking against glass—

instead of mashing him, which
distracts you from finding reasons
to walk by the phone that has taken
a vow of silence sitting in his

plastic, meditating or praying,
which you know you should
be doing, learning the hard work
of stillness, of being alone.

While Praying

I reached through a hole in the air
like a sudden tear in fabric.

I wish I could say I felt bones
or the sandpaper jaw of my dead father
or the pointy edges of a star.

All I felt was more air.

The hole closed,
stitched itself shut.

Sometimes I'll run my hands
along invisible walls
feeling for a seam

like a man in a dark room
searching for a switch.

Land of No Houses

As I drive by the cemetery,
I picture my father in his grave,
hair so long now it is a blanket
covering him, his nails clawed,
curling like a hawk's. A mouse
has found its way into his skull,
looking out the windows
of the eye sockets.
Of course there are worms, moles,
other things—all part of the
neighborhood. I remember

he used to tell me the body
is a house for the spirit;
when we die we just move
to a better new one. I wonder
to what galaxy on what street
he's relocated. I wonder what
his new house looks like.
He used to say we keep
moving from house to house
until we don't need a house
any more. Until our spirit is
beyond the need of walls
and bony furniture.

At this stoplight every time,
without fail, I look over,
forget I am looking,
the car behind honks,
I wave out the window,
turn left to visit my mother
who lives alone now,
whose paint is peeling,

whose shrubs are growing wild,
whose driveway is cracking,
whose roof is leaking.

I bring her mail from
her crooked, splintered box,
pick up her newspaper
thrown near the crumbling
bricks. I let myself in so
she doesn't have to walk
up steps with arthritic knees,
and right about then I think
how my father never said where
we go when we leave our
very last house or what
it is like in the land of
no houses.

I walk through her kitchen,
picture vast empty space
where the weather is always
perfect, the sky always
clear in God's giant head
that is a house of sorts,
I suppose, where I place
my father now because I need
a point of reference.

I walk through the living room
to my mother sitting
in front of the TV, bend down,
kiss her wrinkled cheek.

The Sweetest Part

My father used to say the sweetest part of the peach
is nearest to the pit. He used to say the fruit attains
its fullest flavor there. He used to say that when
hungry in Athens growing up, after his four sisters
and he had drained the soup from the pot, the same
soup stretched to last for a week, he would suck
bones of their marrow to get to the essence.
He used to say that often in the middle,
nearly hidden, waited the treasure. He used to say
he wasn't talking only about food. He took my hand
in his strong hand. He looked down at me as we walked
in the park, as we moved through moments of a day
together, sparrows and robins above us in branches
either chatting or singing.

The Octopus Fisherman

He swings them by the legs
and pounds their heads on rocks,

ignoring us who come to watch
his gut-drenched hands,

their eyes like pebbles
never blinking,

the way they pile up
like empty gloves.

•

The body remembers kisses more than words,
I remember him saying,

my father,
before he kissed me goodbye.

Everything you love you will lose,
he said,

before he disappeared.

•

Everyone leaves, but I linger to look at
the one octopus, too mangled,

the fisherman left. Like a puddle
of jelly it rots,

stinks in sun; flies arrive to feast
on slop,

to bathe and drench themselves
in once living guts.

•

Pick a coffin, choose a last suit,
rub *Kouros,* his favorite cologne

on his face. In his safe a note
telling us not to weep—

...all things die;
even pens run out of ink.

A year later in his jacket pocket
searching for keys, I pull out his comb.

•

Does a raindrop remember sky
from which it falls?

Does a leaf on a branch
want to let go?

Does the river know it is river,
that where it is going is wherever

it is? I finger plastic teeth,
stop in the street and comb my hair.

•

The fisherman drinking beer
in the tavern after...

does he think of thousands
of octopi he's held, does he notice

grime under his nails, does he ever
think loss is the world's way

of saying pay attention? Father,
you were right. On my cheek

       I feel your lips that aren't here.

We Call It Roadkill

This morning on the way to work
a squirrel twitching on the road,
half-mashed by a tire, no doubt,
its fluffy tail flopping side to side
trying to negotiate pain of organs
crushed and bones ground into
dust, and next to it an acorn
which must have been the trophy
of this mission to cross a street
humming with mammoth metal
beasts not stopping for anything.
Right now I'll bet the squirrel
would admit that nut wasn't worth
what layers of shattering plummet
through what's left of its body,
tiny head intact but from the neck
down mostly flat and oozing.
I should slow down, back up,
put the little critter out of its
misery but I'm late and just hope
one day I'm forgiven.
Hunger—and you can clump
to that desire, lust, dreams,
anything that's good and dangled
before our snouts like a prize carrot—
drives us to desperate acts, I'm thinking,
as I zoom past and adjust
the rear view mirror to watch
if the car behind me swerves
or does the job of finishing him off.

My Son and I Explore the Nature of Suffering

He asks why
don't the fish shriek
as we pull them from the water.
Surely it must hurt,
the hook tearing the lips,
the flat eyes eyeing us.
I say they don't have vocal chords,
in other words, no voice.
I say their screams are invisible,
hoping he'll understand better than
inaudible. He says oh you mean they have,
what's it called?—l-a…r-y-n-g-itis?
Something like that, yes, I say,
And what about the worms, he asks.
Are their screams invisible too?
Yes, I say, you understand.
Would we keep fishing if we could hear
their voices, he asks.
Would we still stab these worms?
Good questions, I say.
Yeah, he says, I think it would be hard,
and did you notice, the worms wiggle every time
like they know what is coming?

Ten to One

A worm has ten hearts,
which means they are romantic,
or at least able to love

a lot. You see one
in a robin's beak or on
a sidewalk or in the crater

left by a rock.
You don't think
of them as lovers,

as something that longs
for another of its kind.
Maybe underground

where we never see them
they live secret lives,
tunneling and tunneling

in search of each other
with burning passion.
They can afford

to be struck by Cupid's
arrow without second-guessing
or doubt. Unlike us,

who have just one
that we try not to break
over and over.

Deconstruction

Let's pretend the characters know they are in a story
and they know how the story ends.
Which makes them sad from the beginning.

They move through pages of their lives
looking to the right and left at the air beside
their heads. They are trying to decipher

notes scribbled in the margins.
His character is flawed by some inner conflict
he pretends not to understand,

her character waits hopefully every day
for him to become the man she imagines—
profound, bold, tender.

They marry, have children, divorce,
keep looking for clues, wondering if
the reference to the moon over and over

or the comparison of the future to the way
grass grows means something.
When the reader sleeps, and no one

is looking, the man flips back to before
all the wirings short-circuit.
He sees warnings but ignores them

like the captain of the Titanic nearing
the iceberg. He takes a pick and shovel,
tries to change words which might

alter the chain of events to follow.
When someone opens the book again,
he hides his tools, scrambles back.

They go on page after page, meeting other
lovers, making money, being hurt,
pretending to understand the concept

of God. Sometimes their lines
are flat, uninflected. Sometimes
the setting lacks detail.

They tried screaming long ago
but no one can hear. Even the author is deaf
to their pleas. He has moved on to a new

project. Hopefully, each of them thinks—
this they read between their own lines—
he will not recycle parts of them

to create new characters. He will take a
writing class, jazz his syntax,
make a world bursting with heroic invention.

Since the Divorce

When they're not here
their absence weighs more than
        everyone else's presence.

The body of them not being here
moves toward me through the room
        and sits on my chest.

No one can see this, as my children
not being with me is invisible,
        so my friends wonder

why I act like I'm being
crushed. Melodramatic again,
        they think, rolling their eyes,

not seeing how the absence starts to jump
up and down on me, beat its fists
        on my head, making sure

I feel it fully
until the phone rings and it's their
        voices, wherever they are, saying

they miss me
and can't wait to visit,
        which is when the absence

disappears and I can breathe.
But I hang up and there
        it is again like a sumo wrestler

pushing everyone aside,
throwing furniture out of its path,
        lumbering toward me.

Bees Mating

Two bumblebees in midair join
to make one golf ball-size buzzing.
They bob and weave, suddenly drunk
with each other's zigzagging,
never once separating
though they tumble
into deck furniture,
even bounce off glass
of the sliding door.
It is clear they are mating,
thrilled to have found each other
this warm July day.
They have no idea
I'm watching,
remembering
that first time in the hotel room
as we ripped and clawed,
lost track of time,
even broke the headboard
of the bed,
which didn't stop us.

They sound like more than bees,
the two of them making
this new creature,
a reckless machine
that pinballs off anything in its path,
that refuses, at least for now,
to believe it can ever
fall back to the earth.

Factoid #3: Goldfish Have a Memory Span of Three Seconds

He glides in and out
of a hollow blue castle
eyeing flaky dust
my god-like hand dropped
still floating on the surface.

Am I really hungry?
Or did I just eat?

I can hear him thinking.

Is he angry bumping his head
every third second
against the invisible
wall of time
the way I've walked
into sliding glass doors
after too many martinis?

How did I get here?
Where is my mother?
Was I ever kissed?

Or is he grateful
to escape
the baggage I carry—

the son hugging his G.I. Joe with grape jelly stains
on the plastic cheek, the daughter
looking down at her feet
as the man tries to explain
divorce, saying they'll have two houses

now, two Christmases, two birthdays,
double the toys,
like a used car salesman trying too hard?

He is the only pet
I've had with two
names I alternate:

Today is Monday—he's Lucky.
Tomorrow, Tuesday—he's Cursed.

He looks out from his glass prison.
I look at the sky.

What does he think,
circling the toy diver
whose oxygen tank never empties,
who swims forever
suspended in the same spot
by the castle?

As the Cormorants Are to the Japanese Fishermen, We Are to the Gods

They tie a string around the long neck, loose enough to let the bird
    breathe
and allow small fish to pass through, but tight enough to block
the bigger fish the fishermen want.
The fishermen pull the bird from the water with the help
of a long pole and make it spit the big fish out.
Long ago the fishermen saw the cormorant as a competitor
for fish and devised a strategy.

They say the hunger of one good cormorant can feed a whole family.
The birds dive and dive, apparently happy with the process,
glad to gulp any fish at all, which seem sweet enough.

Still

I have been studying the trees
in my yard, the way they stand,
unflinching,

in their brown armor.
I remember him telling me
to have a thick skin, be tough,

to let insults and hurt bounce off.
It is true, the tree uses bark
to weather cold and storms,

hardly blinks when two lovers
carve their names in its flesh.
But this morning, one bleeds

a sticky sap and I wonder
if it is grieving
for something or someone.

I touch its wound, sniff,
think of my father
gone ten years,

and know that sometimes even
the thickest skin without warning
cannot help but split open.

Not Damaged, Just Altered

I go to the waste basket to throw out the pear,
but my mother says no. I tell her it is all bruised,
it must have fallen or been bumped and sat
for days in the bowl. She says the pear is even
sweeter now, the bruises have grown, have
risen to the pear's surface from beneath
the greenish skin. She takes the pear from
my hand, tenderly unlocking each finger
from the fruit the way I remember the hero
on TV gently slipping the revolver from the
desperate suicidal man's grip after explaining
what a mistake it would be, and she gets out a knife,
slices the pear into wedges, puts one to my lips
and says now taste the bruises.

III

Exploratory Surgery

Say the Lord's workers are fed up,
tired of taking orders all day.
Say they are curious.
They slip God a Mickey in His drink,
then tie Him to a slab and begin.

When they open Him, they find
mountains of bones reaching higher
than Everest or Kilimanjaro.
They find ten billion skulls
lined up polished
on a mantel over a fireplace
stretching a thousand miles.
Laughter and weeping pour out
of Him like air
from a punctured balloon.

They open doors to rooms:
in one a collection of dolls—
Einstein doll, Mozart doll,
Ghandi doll, and more—
maybe His best creations.
In another room
a huge movie screen
on which He watches
the reality show of our lives.
In another a bar where He goes
to get away from the stresses
of being God, where He drinks
and stares at His own face
in the mirror behind the counter.

But one room won't open,
is locked, is where the workers

decide God must keep the Devil
in chains. Maybe God
abuses him at night, plays
torture games.
Maybe God forces him
to write daily scripts for the
reality show but takes credit
as the author Himself.

They pick the lock,
throw in metal-cutting pliers,
leave the door ajar—then seal
God back up and at their stations
pretend to work, as from the corners
of their eyes they spy God
slumped on the floor,
starting to stretch, yawn,
wake up.

The Voice Inside

The only good thing after I ruptured
my Achilles is being able to ride
on one of those motorized carts
in the grocery. I had always wondered
what it would be like to press a button—
zip here, zip there, weaving
up and down aisles through traffic,
tossing a head of lettuce into the front
attached basket then making my way
toward breads and cakes, toward the
lady with a plate of toothpick-stabbed
free sample egg rolls and onto the meats
where filets and porterhouses smile
their bloody smiles behind windows,
happy not to be chuck roasts or burger
crammed in cellophane. Not so much
the feeling of driving but the feeling
of noticing the way eyes see me
is what I wanted
and now I have a reason.

The old man with a cane deliberating
over crackers tips his golf cap,
the bald guy who never smiles
wearing the blood-spattered coat
carrying a salmon like a baby
in his arms grins, two tight-
skirted women in high heels
in a hurry on their break
let me go before them at the deli
though their number is 9
and mine is 10. People soften
when they see someone damaged,

somewhere buried in their bodies
a tiny voice recording whispers:
that could be you,
it will be you one day. Even if
faces don't show it the voice
starts programmed
to come on with a switch wired
from the eyes to the mechanism hidden
somewhere behind
the liver near the spleen.

As I cruise through cheeses and milk
I know this because the voice
almost daily whispers—you can't
escape hearing—everywhere you look
people with bodies breaking down
for a variety of reasons. Even on TV,
every other story shows mangling,
withering, flesh-petals falling
piece by piece. But the thing
about the voice is it fades
in seconds, doesn't play
over and over, which means we hurry
along forgetting we live in a body
that will betray us in the end.

In the check-out, everyone moves
aside, lets me pass to the front,
a tattooed biker even offers to empty
my cart. I imagine God's technician
watching from his workshop in space.
He smiles, pleased that the voice inside
so much flesh down here works,
the wiring correctly wired. He is
working hard, trying to invent a voice

that speaks louder, lingers longer.
He takes one last look—
as the biker with a scar on his chin
and no front teeth
places my last item, a jar of olives,
onto the conveyer belt and pats me
on the back—then turns, hunches
over his desk, adjusts a knob
on his microscope, gets back to work.

Weighing

Shaving,
I wonder how much the mirror
would weigh

with nothing in it.

I step away,
step back,
touch glass with fingertips.

Every day I do this,

looking at the face
I've earned
with countless joys and griefs.

One day I will shave and do

the ritual not knowing
it is the last time.
Every morning I am rehearsing

saying goodbye to myself.

Arthritis

Pain in the spine and sides:
        easy to diagnose the problem.
I'm sure it is ghost birds
        who peck at seeds of every moment I lived

but was not awake to
        fluttering behind the bony cage of my ribs.
Inevitable, aging we say.
        But the body knows we squander

seconds, minutes, hours, days—
        leafing through magazines
full of photos of people
        we imagine being,

rich and famous;
        or staring at a TV screen;
or driving from point A to point B
        to feel we're getting somewhere—

instead of walking across the room
        and taking the one we love in our arms,
looking into their eyes;
        or stepping out into cool air,

gazing up at clouds,
        how they form miracle images
on a giant canvas for us;
        or even sitting silently

listening to the heart's echo
        in the deep well of the body
where those birds fill us, fighting
        each other over those seeds—

which hurts inside—
    which we name,
thinking we know all about living
    and why it hurts to grow old.

Stubborn Ode

Not now I say to the sparrow proudly
not singing on the branch outside
my window. Not now to the tree
standing in defiance of wind lashing,
cold descending around it.
Not now I say to the worms deep
under ground fighting over blankets
of dirt to keep warm. Not now
to the day with its harp of ribs
it strums trying to persuade me.
I am listening to the sound
the faucet makes dripping. I am
trying to repair the broken toy
of my brain, to understand
why truth fits too snugly
calling itself fiction.
Not now even to God
screwing stars deeper into
the sky tightening the beyond
to the present. Not now I say
to the sparrow once again
although I'm in awe of how
he dodges bullets of rain.

My Kid and God

My kid lives in a virtual world
where people are controlled
by pushing buttons.
He sits in front of the computer
all day, like God
who decides men's fates.
It is more fun and less complicated,
I suppose, than *really* being thrown out
at the plate when he should have held
at third or *actually* mowing a lawn
and sweating. Less disappointment,
no screaming coach, no burning drops
in the eyes. He even manipulates
the phantom husband
and wife on the screen who bicker
then make up. Sometimes he puts
the man in another house
with a new woman, sometimes he puts
the woman with another woman.

I understand how addictive
it must be and why God must enjoy
being who He is. You never hear
of The Almighty feeling lonely
or wondering if He can save
enough for His kid's
tuition. He doesn't bother
taking out trash or gulping
daily vitamins. He is never turned
down for a date, never has to worry
about plucking His eyebrows.
It's more fun to watch everyone
else skin their knees, get dirty,

disgusted, worn out. So what
if it is a perfect, sunny July day,
the birds practicing their arias
in the trees and now the jingle
of the Good Humor man
rounding the corner in his truck?
There are tidal waves to stir up,
murders, births, wars to create.
If suddenly rain should fall
or a heart breaks that isn't supposed
to break, all my kid and God
have to do is press *Restart.*

This Moment Like Any Other

The taxidermist is working late
rereading the chapter
on facial expression,
      the unfinished head
lying on its side.

At home
his wife is stirring martinis,
      staring at the clock.

Meanwhile, the TV shows a country
blowing up,
      then a commercial about raising IQ's
with meditation.

A man in a suit goes door to door,
      inquiring if anyone can spare
a bullet for him to bite;

      he thought he was over the fact
      that his son was shot in Iraq.

The taxidermist tries to scratch
between his shoulder blades,
      doesn't know it is where
we all once had wings.

      The wife turns off the TV.
The taxidermist keeps trying
to reach the itchy spot.
      The man in the suit's tears

on his cheeks trickle back
      up into his eyes
whose lashes sew the eyes shut.

No Nirvana

The Buddhist priest holds a cell phone
to his ear. Like a big baby
in diapers, he is cursing loudly
into the small gadget
as he stands at a bus stop.

Maybe he is angry at God
who stranded him,
who promised to pick him up
if he waited in the right place
long enough.

Maybe he is chewing God out
for not delivering the bliss
as promised after all those
meditations.

Maybe he is reminding God
of the times he starved,
denied himself even a peek
of the billboard next to the highway
with the twenty-foot woman
in a bikini.

Maybe he is telling God off,
tired like the rest of us
of young boys dying,
and even more of men
making boys believe
they'll be heroes.

He snaps shut the phone,
scratches his bald head,
opens it, presses buttons,
starts cursing again.

Day of Rest

Today I'd rather argue
about the way
steaks should be cooked
than about the war in Iraq.
I'd rather watch the squirrels
leap from tree to tree
in a mid-air ballet
than turn on the TV
to the latest toll of dead
soldiers, never mind
civilian mothers,
fathers, brothers,
sisters. I'd rather
sit on my stoop
and wave
at the passing cars
than read the newspaper
advertising everything
we shouldn't want
even for free.
I'd rather watch my son
shoot baskets,
my daughter ride her bike,
than invite sadness
and fury
and the frustration
of knowing stupidity
sometimes wins.
I'd rather watch
my woman finishing
what I started,
pulling the last
of the weeds,
looking beautiful,

making little grunts
as she stoops,
and tell my neighbor
who sits beside me
claiming he knows
secrets of tenderizing
meat that he's crazy
than weep, weep,
weep.

Factoid #4: Children Laugh about 400 Times a Day While Adults Laugh on Average Only 15 Times a Day

That's why I go around following children.
I wait till they laugh then catch their laughs in a net.

It's not hard; they're like butterflies floating.
I take the laughs home, dump them on the table,

one by one swallow them, filling me.
They go down easy, like clams on the half-shell,

and they taste like air. The rest of the day I belch them
up, feeling like a kid again, everyone saying

"What's so funny? What's so damn funny?"
Sometimes I go to parks: swings, monkey-bars,

teeter-totters—fertile ground for laugh hunting.
Summer is best, lots of children everywhere.

I catch enough that I store laughs in my closet
by the hundreds. I need a supply

for winter and certain days when being
an adult hurts too much. I admit

I'm addicted. My own children laugh
less and less. They want to be adults,

and think laughing is kid stuff.
So this poem is for them,

for when they're grown and starved
for a laugh but so empty they'd settle

even for a smile. *Picture me behind bushes*
spying on neighbor kids, jumping out

at the first sign of a giggle with my net.
Picture me hoarding them in drawers,

under the bed, in jars the way we trapped fireflies
long ago. See me slurping them down

till I'm drunk with laughs, dancing around
the room with a lampshade on my head.

Pick up your own net
or try to find the child who plays

hide and seek inside
that you thought was lost,

who this very second is peeking
from behind one of your ribs.

Graffiti

Carved on the bathroom stall wall
in gray metal,
the words, *Love Me,* like an island
surrounded by cruder scratchings
of men or boys who sat where I sit
in this truck stop off I-80.
A limerick, phone numbers,
even a stick figure man with
disproportionately huge genitals
bigger than his whole body
like the Samoan sculptures in the museum.
But this command,
so primal, blunt, as if spoken
by a lover told he's not loved anymore,
almost begging, or a belt-whipped child
cowering in a corner barely able to say
the words through quivering lips—
no time to get fancy with metaphors, rhyme,
just *Love Me*—
makes me carve those same words
into God's stony heart,
which must be a wall,
hieroglyphics, scribbled, scarred,
hacked with every kind of prayer.

Geometry

Everywhere things are beginning for people:
kisses, ideas, the first buds of love

sprouting, the tiny almost unnoticeable cracks
in love's granite. One person's starting line

is another person's finish. Today, ten thousand
people will vanish and their small replacements

will bring someone joy. So when I sit on my
stoop and look at the sun going down,

I know it is rising for someone
who looks at it thinking it is setting

for someone somewhere else. Everywhere
parts of people are dying inside them

and parts are being born like happy tumors.
Clouds stitch themselves together

with invisible string stretching
around the globe like rubber bands

around a basketball as someone pictures
me on this stoop looking up, though

he, like me, just sees what floats above him.
We will never meet, he and I, dots

on a graph that will never touch,
but each of us draws a line toward the other,

a perfect line that links us forever,
a line that proves no dot is ever alone,

ever separate without another dot.

No More Same Old Silly Love Songs

When the radio in my car broke I started to notice the trees.
I began to stop exaggerating the color of leaves,
how their reds and oranges need no wordy embellishment.
I started to open my window and smell the wet pavement
after morning rain. Crows on the phone line,
their blackness and stubborn dignity. I even noticed my hands
gripping the wheel, the small dark hairs, the skin,
the knuckles and the perfect blue veins.

Factoid #5: Crocodiles Swallow Stones
to Help Them Dive Deeper

I close my eyes and see my teenage son surprising me,
letting me hold his hand as we cross the busy street downtown.
I play the recording I keep in a vault behind my ribs
of my daughter laughing so hard she can't breathe
that time she fell in a pile of leaves.
I gulp and hold my breath. I open the ribcage like a door.
I swim inside and push the lungs to more easily get to
my father's face, eyes closed never to open again
on the hospital bed, to my mother after too long missing,
finding her in the lady's room weeping.
I move the liver, lift the spleen. I find there curled up
the light bulb burning out over my head
my first Christmas alone after the divorce,
the phone not ringing in the dark. I touch the memory;
it twitches. I stare a long time at their Disney toothbrushes
in plastic mugs near the sink. At his ball cap on the bedpost.
Her crayons. Yes, I slide deeper through the muck
till I bump against the me on my roof,
listening to the crickets; waiting and waiting
for the moon like God's face, telling myself
if it joins me I'm forgiven, if not more penance.
I swim a little further, behind the stomach, around the spine
near the heart. I come up for air. Somewhere
in its reptilian brain the crocodile knows the surface
is sufficient. It can find plenty to eat there, it can
survive. Stones taste gritty, mossy, dirty. Sometimes bitter.
And yet. I think of Jonnie's impish grin.
I think of Ali's hair.

Message

Sometimes you stop in the middle of a moment:
put the book down or just stand in the room
forgetting where you were headed.

Marble-still, you feel like a chandelier
waiting to be lit;

or like a dog whose hearing hears
what you can't, you lean toward eternity,
straining for the evidence.

I Go Out Walking With My Dead Friends

Plants in a kitchen window,
lights on here and there.
Soon the fireflies.
They tell me to stop wasting time
like a talent. They say it is a river
flowing both ways.
Sure, I say, then offer them a puff
of my cigar. They say go inside
and unlock the curved trunk of a body,
someone's you love. Loosen the rib
straps and slide a hand into the space
where he or she keeps those things
closest to the heart. Watch the face
for signs of wakefulness. Let your
fingertips brush the inner lining.
You don't want them to know
what you are doing.
Nothing else matters, they say.
But it is too early, no one is asleep,
I tell them. Besides, we hug sometimes,
now and then even notice each other's eyes.
They get quiet and look down at their feet.
I kick some pebbles. They tsk.
We pass more houses, not talking,
listen to the crickets.

Acknowledgments

Grateful acknowledgement is made to the following publications in which some of these poems first appeared:

Atlanta Review: "Day of Rest"

Babel Fruit: "I Go Out Walking With My Dead Friends," "Instead of Writing a Poem About Writing a Poem, I Step Outside and Smell the Air," "Pressing Buttons"

The Chaffin Journal: "Factoid #1: The Hummingbird is the Only Bird that Can Fly Backwards"

The Chimaera: "Arthritis," "Message"

Dark Sky: "Hunger," "While Praying"

Ekakshara: "The Sweetest Part"

5 AM: "Factoid #3: Goldfish Have a Memory Span of Three Seconds"

The Georgia Review: "Workers for the Lord" (also previously appeared through Main Street Rag Press)

Jelly Bucket: "The Octopus Fisherman"

Poet Lore: "Not Damaged, Just Altered"

The Portland Review: "The Body of Christ," "The Egg"

Slant: "Factoid #2: Men Are Six Times More Likely To Be Struck by Lightning Than Women"

Beyond the Bones was a finalist for the 2009 FutureCycle Poetry Book Prize.

Book design: cover and artwork by Carole Carpathios (cantoncarp@aol.com); flourishes and technicals by Donna Overall (donnaoverall@bellsouth.net); typography by Diane Kistner (dkistner@futurecycle.org).

THE FUTURECYCLE POETRY BOOK PRIZE

All full-length volumes of poetry published by FutureCycle Press
in a given calendar year are considered for the annual
FutureCycle Poetry Book Prize. This allows us to consider
each submission on its own merits, outside of the context of a contest.
Too, the judges see the finished book, which will have benefitted from
the beautiful book design and strong editorial gloss we are famous for.

The book ranked the best in judging is announced as the prize-winner in
the subsequent year. There is no fixed monetary award; instead, the
winning poet receives an honorarium of 20% of the total net royalties
from all poetry books and chapbooks the press sold online in the year
the winning book was published. The winner is also accorded the honor
of judging the next year's competition.

.

www.ingramcontent.com/pod-product-compliance
Lightning Source LLC
Chambersburg PA
CBHW070008100426
42741CB00012B/3151